# MAD

## ABOUT

# DAD

## "THE USUAL GANG OF IDIOTS"

Introductions by DAVID SHAYNE

### RUTLEDGE HILL PRESS®
NASHVILLE, TENNESSEE

A Division of Thomas Nelson, Inc.
www.ThomasNelson.com

Published by Rutledge Hill Press, a Division of Thomas Nelson, Inc.,
P.O. Box 141000, Nashville, Tennessee, 37214.

1-4016-0149-9

Printed in the United States of America
04 05 06 07 08 — 5 4 3 2 1

# To Dad–

I've clocked the motion of the wind,
And looked at my barometer;
I've watched the movements of the clouds,
And studied my thermometer;
No matter how I check my charts
And scan the skies of blue,
I know that I shall never find
A hot air mass like you!

Artist: George Woodbridge    Writer: Frank Jacobs

MAD ABOUT DAD

# Introduction

~~~

**T**his isn't just a book *for* a very special man...
this is a book *about* a very special man!

The man who imparted poignant words of wisdom
such as, "I'm watching the game, go ask your Mother"
and "No one belches at the dinner table...except
for me."

The man who waited until the car was at least a
good 100 feet out of the driveway on family vacations
before angrily threatening to turn it around and
go home.

This is a book about *you*, Dad.

# The Lighter Side of COMPETITION

Artist & writer: Dave Berg

# If Kids Behaved Like Their Fathers

**W**e keep hearing a lot about the "Generation Gap" these days...that children and adults have nothing in common...that young people live in a world of their own and never listen to older folks...and that things would be a lot better if kids would only behave! Behave like who...their parents? Well, let's just see how much better things would be if kids became real "chips off the old blocks" and followed the examples of the older generation.

# The Stockbroker's Son

Artist: Jack Rickard    Writer: Frank Jacobs

# MAD's Snappy Answers to a Stupid Question

Artist & writer: Al Jaffee

# And Baby Makes (Gulp!) Three

Before you became a father, you had it pretty good.

Your TV wasn't permanently tuned to Nickelodeon. You ate dinner in peace. When you walked down the halls you didn't stub your toes on stray toys. And Mom was never too tired to . . . you know.

Yet for some reason that escapes logic and reason, you thought it might be a good idea to start a family.

Nine months later, there you were in the hospital room, waiting for the bundle of joy to arrive. You were dressed like an extra from *ER,* which was good because the mask covered the look of sheer terror plastered on your sweating face.

You were about to take on an awesome responsibility: the life of a child. You'd have to clothe it, feed it, pay for its braces, schooling, and property damage, and dedicate your very being to it.

But first, you'd have to learn the dirtiest job of all—changing diapers!

Ecch! Welcome to fatherhood!

# One Fine Day in the Maternity Ward

Artist & writer: Don Martin

# MAD Salutes Some Legendary Dads...

Artist: Jack Davis
Writer: Duck Edwing

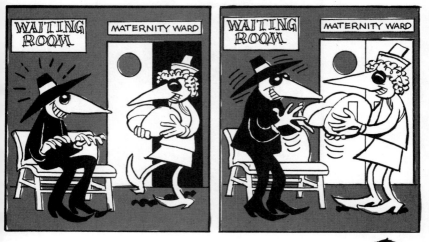

# You Know You're REALLY A PARENT When...

... the most dreaded event of the year is no longer "Income Tax" time, but that "Pre-Christmas Toy-Assembly" section!

Artist: Paul Cocker, Jr.
Writer: Phil Hahn & Jack Hanrahan

# You Know You're REALLY A PARENT When...

... you're asked to solve some "New Math" problems, and it suddenly dawns on you that you never really understood the "Old Math"!

# You Know You're REALLY A PARENT When...

. . . you discover you're brushing your teeth with "Pimple Cream"!

# You Know You're REALLY A PARENT When...

... you never buy anything for the house that isn't plastic, vinyl, or cast iron!

# You Know You're
# REALLY A PARENT When...

... you discover that your alarm clock has been broken for five years, and you hadn't even noticed!

# You Know You're REALLY A PARENT When...

. . . you suddenly find that your electric bill comes to three dollars less than you paid for batteries for toys that month!

# What is a Parent?

**R**emember 1971?

Nixon was president. The nation was at war. The economy was sinking. Bad times.

On the plus side, you still had all of your hair and your gut hadn't started spilling out over your belt yet.

This piece first ran in 1971 and it didn't have much nice to say about Dads. But when you think about it, you were only a kid then, so this isn't really an article about what a lousy bum *you* are — it's an article about what a lousy bum *grandpa* is!

Please keep that in mind before you cut off the allowance, okay, Dad?

Artist: Sergio Aragones   Writer: Tom Koch

**BETWEEN** the time your kindergarten teacher introduces you to hand puppets and the time your army sergeant introduces you to hand grenades, you can expect to waste about fifteen years hollering across the generation gap at a couple of creatures called "Parents." Unfortunately, it is futile to holler at Parents for the same reasons it is futile to holler at French waiters: (1) They don't understand your language; (2) They're not even listening; and (3) They're usually hollering at you louder than you're hollering at them.

**IT'S EASY** to spot Parents in a crowd. They're the ones yelling at the little leaguer who dropped the fly ball in order to make sure he feels humiliated enough. They're the ones pushing the supermarket carts loaded with the newest, awful-tasting stuff advertised as "vital to your growing child's health!" They're the ones leaving the porch light on so their teenagers can't do whatever teenagers supposedly do on dark porches. And they're the ones circulating the petition to have *Gray's Anatomy* banned from the local library as smut.

**THE WORST** thing about Parents is that they're inconsistent. They believe in democracy, but not to the point of giving you a voice in what you eat for dinner. They understand inflation, but they don't understand why you need a bigger allowance than they got twenty-five years ago. They're all for driver's education, but they don't think passing the course qualifies you to drive the family car. And they advocate free speech, but they'd better not catch you using any around the house.

**TO GET ALONG** with your male Parent, you must first appreciate that he embodies many of the qualities of other great men. He has the quiet patience of Eldridge Cleaver, the unquestioning trust of J. Edger Hoover, the forgiving nature of Spiro Agnew, the sense of justice of Mao Tse-Tung, the open-minded flexibility of Lester Maddox, the boundless generosity of Vito Genovese, the disarming warmth of Don Rickles, the humane understanding of Mayor Daley, and the mature approach of Captain Kangaroo.

**EVERY SO OFTEN,** the male Parent will make a stab at communicating with his offspring. The subjects he most enjoys discussing during these heart-to-heart chats include: your low marks at school, your spotty attendance record at church, your weak showing in athletics, your poor attitude toward a career in dentistry, and your unreasonable feelings about his boss's ugly daughter. The subjects he least enjoys discussing include: his latest hassle with the Internal Revenue Service, his grounds for draft deferment during World War II, his inability to quit smoking, and his close association with every bookie in town (and every secretary in his office).

**ALL IN ALL,** Parents just never seem to get with it. Because they lack a strong social conscience, they've continued to earn enough money to feed, clothe, and house you to this point in your life. Because they insist upon treating you as a child, they've managed to prevent you from accidentally killing yourself at least a dozen times before you got to this point. And because of their stodgy view of today's changing values, they've succeeded in keeping you toiling away in school when you could have become an accomplished Greenwich Village panhandler by now.

**STILL,** with all of their shortsightedness and lack of understanding, Parents do serve one vital function. Just think of the terrible blisters you'd get from practicing your guitar too long…and the diamond needles you'd wear out from playing your Janice Joplin records all night…and the gas money you'd waste from revving up your hot-rod in the driveway if there were no Parents around to emit that familiar, annoying cry:

### "STOP MAKING ALL THAT INFERNAL RACKET!"

# The Lighter Side of **WISDOM**

Artist & writer: Dave Berg

MAD ABOUT DAD

# On a Saturday Afternoon

Artist & writer: Don Martin

# The Lighter Side of **BABYSITTING**

Artist & writer: Dave Berg

# A Father's Day Card From a Foreign Correspondent

Artist: George Woodbridge
Writer: Frank Jacobs

I've covered riots in Berlin
    and fighting in Algiers;
I've tangled with Katanga tribes
    and dodged their poison spears;
I've seen the savage Red Chinese;
    I've braved the atom bomb;
But nothing, Dad, will ever beat
    Those fights you have with Mom!

THE SUPER DADDY LOVES HIS KIDS—so much, in fact, that he takes them everywhere—even to the arcade! The Super Daddy does this because he's deeply committed to his child's personal growth and emotional development. That's why he sticks Junior between two video games for several hours—because it builds character!!

Artist: Tom Bunk    Writer: Sean Eisenporth

# The Kid Stays in the Picture... Too Bad for You

~~~~

**Y**ou know, it wasn't so long ago that I was just a little tyke. Those were the good ol' days, weren't they?

You'd let work pile up on your desk to skip out of the office early and take me to a day game at the stadium.

Instead of mowing the lawn you'd watch Saturday morning cartoons with me while we both ate way too many bowls of sugar-covered cereal.

And forget balancing the checkbook or paying the bills — not when you could play video games with me all night.

Hmmm... I think I finally understand what Mom means when she says she had *two* children.

# A MAD Look at Video Cameras

Artist & writer: Sergio Aragones

# The Lighter Side of SUMMER CAMP

Artist & writer: Dave Berg

# The Lighter Side of CAR OWNERS

Artist & writer: Dave Berg

 MAD ABOUT DAD

# A Father's Day Card From a Doctor

Artist: George Woodbridge
Writer: Frank Jacobs

Your pancreas is calcified;
    Your fibroplasts are clotting;
And near your seventh vertebra
    A spinal disc is rotting;
Your liver's twice its normal size;
    One lung is turning gray;
I hope your life is filled with joy
    This happy Father's Day!

# The Lighter Side of LITTLE LEAGUE

Artist & writer: Dave Berg

# The Lighter Side of **NERDS**

Artist & writer: Dave Berg

# The Lighter Side of **COMPETITION**

Artist & writer: Dave Berg

MAD ABOUT DAD

# A Bedtime Story as told by

Artist: Wallace Wood   Writer: Frank Jacobs

Now that good-old-fashioned spankings have passed from the American scene, about the only things that influence a child on his father's knee these days are the bedtime stories he hears. MAD has investigated this situation, however, and we have discovered that most fathers aren't content with

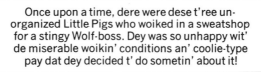

Once upon a time, dere were dese t'ree un-organized Little Pigs who woiked in a sweatshop for a stingy Wolf-boss. Dey was so unhappy wit' de miserable woikin' conditions an' coolie-type pay dat dey decided t' do sometin' about it!

SOAP

# a "job-conscious" father

merely telling these famous fairy tales the way they were originally written. No, indeed! The modern father adds a little extra to these stories. To show you how much extra, try this one...

De foist Little Pig wrote up a list of grievances on a sheet of paper, and took it to his exploiting, capitalist Wolf-boss . . . but de Wolf jus' huffed, an' he puffed, an' he tore up de sheet of paper . . .

**Paper! Bah!** This is what I do to lists of grievances! Now get back to work!

De second Little Pig decided to picket, so he made a wooden sign an' marched up an' down in front of de sweatshop. But de Wolf jus' huffed, an' he puffed, an' he busted de sign to pieces!

**Wood! Bah!** This is what I do to wooden picket signs! Now get back to work!

An' so de T'ree Little Pigs went back to woik wit' a Union Contract, an' double-time for over-time, an' holidays wit' pay, an' vacations wit' pay, an' compensation, an' hospitalization, an' coffee breaks, an' lots of other fringe benefits. An' pretty soon, de stingy Wolf-boss went bankrupt an' hadda go out of business!

An' de moral of de story is: In Unions dere is strength!

# The MAD Like... Love... Hate Book

Artist: Paul Cocker, Jr.    Writers: Frank Jacobs & Marylyn Ippolito

### Don't You LIKE...

... having a father who is very interested in your schoolwork?

### Don't You LOVE...

... conning him into doing your Math homework for you?

## Don't You HATE...

... getting a failing mark on the Math homework he did?

# The Lighter Side of COMPETITION

Artist & writer: Dave Berg

# The Lighter Side of **GUIDANCE**

Artist & writer: Dave Berg

MAD ABOUT DAD

# Children are Better Teen Than Heard

**T**his is the part of the book about being a father during the Teenage Years, or as you might call them, the *Will-You-Shut-That-@#!%#$-Music-Off-Your-Mother-and-I-Are-Trying-to-Get-Some-Sleep-and-No,-You-Can't-Borrow-the-Car-on-Friday-Night-to-Drive-around-with-Your-Hoodlum-Friends-Dressed-in-Those-Ridiculous-Tattered-Clothes-with-Those-Awful-Haircuts-Doing-Lord-Knows-What-with-Lord-Knows-Who-until-All-Hours-of-the-%$!@#-Night!* Years.

You know, now that I think about it, those are the years the typical dad's hair starts to go gray.

Coincidence?

# The Lighter Side of **TEENAGERS**

Artist & writer: Dave Berg

MAD ABOUT DAD

# The Lighter Side of **PREPAREDNESS**

Artist & writer: Dave Berg

# The Lighter Side of **APPRECIATION**

Artist & writer: Dave Berg

# The Lighter Side of **HIGH SCHOOL**

Artist & writer: Dave Berg

MAD ABOUT DAD

# The Lighter Side of GIFTS

Artist & writer: Dave Berg

# The Lighter Side of **THE TELEPHONE**

Artist & writer: Dave Berg

 MAD ABOUT DAD

# The Lighter Side of BABY SITTING

Artist & writer: Dave Berg

MAD ABOUT DAD    97

# A Father's Day Card
# From a Peace Corp Member

Artist: George Woodbridge
Writer: Frank Jacobs

When I was young, you bullied me
    And filled me with defiance;
And so I joined the Peace Corps, Dad,
    To get some self-reliance;
Out here, I've learned to be a man;
    I'm more mature now, really;
I'm sending home my seven wives;
    I hope you speak Swahili!

# The Lighter Side of PARENTS

Artist & writer: Dave Berg

My boyfriend and I are **going someplace** and he's **picking me up!** So whatever you do, **don't embarrass me** in front of him!

Don't **SAY** anything **dumb**!..! Don't **DO** anything **dumb**!..! Don't **BE dumb!** Understand?!

# The Lighter Side of WINNING

Artist & writer: Dave Berg

MAD ABOUT DAD

# The Lighter Side of **PARENTS**

Artist & writer: Dave Berg

# The Lighter Side of **COMMUNICATING**

Artist & writer: Dave Berg

 MAD ABOUT DAD

 **MAD ABOUT DAD**

# The Lighter Side of GOING STEADY

Artist & writer: Dave Berg

How can two punk kids like you **go steady?** You don't even know what life and love are **all about!**

Children of today are **much** better informed than when **you** were a child. Things like **television** and **improved education methods** have accelerated us **beyond** our **chronological years!**

MAD ABOUT DAD

# The Lighter Side of **PARENTS**

Artist & writer: Dave Berg

When I was a **teenager,** it **bugged** me that my parents **didn't understand me?**

So I made a vow that when I had teenage children, I would do my **darndest** to try to understand **them!** And that's exactly what happened! Today, I **thoroughly understand** my **teenage children!**

**MAD ABOUT DAD**

# A Sentimental Moment for You, Dad

**W**ow! Dads have really been taking it on the chin for the last 113 pages.

You guys have been portrayed as goofy, uncaring, clumsy, foolish, plaid-pant-wearing, irrational, temperamental, child-dropping mouth-breathers who are entirely unfit to take care of themselves, much less a small child.

This book was some gift, huh? Maybe next year I'll just give you some arsenic and you can get it over with quick.

Anyway, since this book is almost at an end, I'd like to say something about how much you mean to me, how much you've taught me, how much you've helped me grow into the person I am today.

I'd like to say all that, but a) there really isn't much room left on the page and b) you taught me never to lie.

Besides, there are still so many insults left to hurl in the years to come.

Speaking of which, turn the page . . .

# The Lighter Side of PARENTS

Artist & writer: Dave Berg

# The Lighter Side of THOUGHTFULNESS

Artist & writer: Dave Berg

# The Lighter Side of HOBBIES

Artist & writer: Dave Berg

MAD ABOUT DAD

# Fathers are Two-Time Losers

**D**on't think your Old Man has it made. In fact, he's really gotten the lousy end of the stick. How come? Well, between the time he was a kid and the time he became a parent, something terrible happened . . . mainly, "child psychology!" Years ago, a kid had to worry about his parents' feelings. Now, when he's old enough to get his licks, he has to bow to the psychology books that tell him: "Consider the child, above all."

Artist: George Woodbridge    Writer: Stan Hart

# When it comes to REPORT CARDS...

**AS A BOY,** Irving Blootz would shudder whenever he brought home a bad report card. It meant he would be giving up fun time to concentrate on schoolwork.

**TODAY,** a father must take total responsibility for his son's performance in school. So, Irving still shudders at the sight of a bad report card. It means he'll be giving up "golf time" to bone up on the "New Math" so he can concentrate on helping Junior with his schoolwork—if it's convenient for Junior.

# When it comes to
# ATHLETIC ACHIEVEMENTS...

**WHENEVER** Bob Mushblech was benched during a ball game, he would suffer terrible embarrassment and long for a quick, painless death. After all, what son wanted his father to think he was a failure?

**IN TODAY'S** "child-oriented" society, a father is judged by his son's accomplishments. So, Bob suffers terrible embarrassment and longs for a quick, painless death when his son sits out a game. After all, what man wants his friends to think he's a failure?

# When it comes to
# HAVING HIS OWN ROOM...

**AS A BOY,** Lou Greppse was forced to share a room with his four brothers. And so, he couldn't wait to grow up, get married, buy a home and finally have a room of his own.

**BECAUSE** psychiatrists claim that locking the parent's door might symbolize rejection to an impressionable youngster, Lou now has a room of his own with a steady stream of little intruders trooping through. They include his own four kids, their thirty friends, and two strangers who were just passing by.

# When it comes to
# FAMILY CONVERSATION...

**WHENEVER** his parents were engaged in conversation, Phil Finster would have to sit quietly and listen—bored stiff. He couldn't interject anything because children were supposed to be "seen and not heard".

**PSYCHOLOGY BOOKS** tell us: "It is essential that parents show an interest in their children." So, Phil sits like death itself while his son goes on endlessly about his pal's ant collection. Today, it's parents who are supposed to be "seen and not heard".

# The Lighter Side of **LITTLE LEAGUE**

Artist & writer: Dave Berg

 **MAD ABOUT DAD**

**I**n the beginning, Adam and Eve had two sons, Cain and Abel...and thus formed the world's first family. And from them, mankind received a wonderful legacy and a code of living that has served families for generations, namely: (a) Don't talk to snakes and (b) If your brother bugs you, hit him with a rock. But if some things remain the same, others change— particularly in the U.S. in the twentieth century. So join us now as *MAD Magazine* examines...

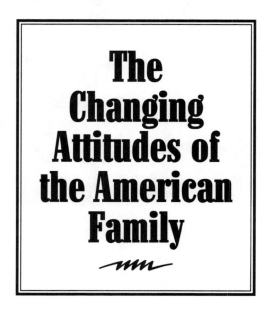

# The Changing Attitudes of the American Family

Artist: George Woodbridge    Writer: Larry Siegel

# MONEY...

**Early 1900s** — In those days, there was only one thing to do with money: Save it.

**Middle 1900s** — Well, the son did exactly as his father had advised and put the $5,000 in a bank! Then, forty years later on *his* son's eighteenth birthday...

> Son, 40 years ago, my Father gave me a check for **$5000** on my **18th birthday**! I wanted to buy a **Stutz Bearcat**, but he advised me to put it in the **bank**, and I **did**! Now, that $5000 has grown to **$13,000** . . . and I'd like to give that money to **you** on this, **your** 18th birthday!

> Waste your money on a **car?** That's **foolish** and **irresponsible**, Son! **Be thrifty! Save it!**

> **Thanks**, Dad! I think I'll buy a **Rolls Royce**!

**...and today** — Well, the son obeyed his father's wishes and put the $13,000 in the bank. Then, twenty-six years later, the son told the story to *his* son and gave him the money, now grown to $20,000...

> **Here**, Son, and there's a lesson in **thrift** you can learn from that original $5000! Do you know what $20,000 can **buy** today?

> But if your Grandpa had **bought** a Stutz Bearcat instead of putting that $5000 in the bank, what would **you** have **now** . . .?

> One thing **I can't stand** is a smart-ass kid!!

> Yeah! About what **$5000** could buy **65 years ago**!

> An antique automobile worth about **$45,000**!!

# RESPECT...

**Early 1900s** — In this period, the family was ruled by a dictatorial, powerfully built, strong masculine presence — the American Father.

**Middle 1900s**—With a growing permissiveness and independence within the family structure, the Father, in an effort to be fair, no longer commanded. Now, he asked. The only trouble was...nobody answered.

Hey, gang! What say we visit **Granny** in **New Jersey?** Okay, **scratch** that! What say she visits **us from** New Jersey? Okay, then it's **settled!** We'll meet her **half-way,** like in the **middle** of the **Lincoln Tunnel,** and **wave!**

Now, what say I buy her a **car** first . . . so she doesn't get **killed?!?**

**...and today**—Nowadays, in a sense, we have returned to some old fashioned values. Once again, the family is ruled by a dictatorial, powerfully built, strong masculine presence, mainly the American Mother!

TODAY, WE WILL VISIT MY MOTHER IN PHILADELPHIA! IS THAT CLEAR?

Yes, Agatha!

Yes, Mother!

Yes, Sir!

# The Lighter Side of **MODERN TECHNOLOGY**

Artist & writer: Dave Berg

Daddy, what makes a **light bulb** light up when you turn on the switch?

Okay! I guess I'm **never** too busy to answer a **good** question!

When you turn on the switch, you complete a **circuit** which allows electricity to flow through the **filament** inside the light bulb, causing it to **heat up** and **glow brightly!**

**P**arents are the ones responsible for the "Generation Gap," and here's why: Whenever you tell them something, no matter how important it is to you, it becomes nothing more than a lead-in for them to zap you with criticism. Right? In other words, parents are the acknowledged masters of the "non-sequitur," which is Latin for "saying what they want, no matter what you say to them!" Here's what we mean by...

# Parental Non-Sequiturs

Artist: Paul Coker, Jr.    Writer: Stan Hart

**WHAT YOU SAY TO YOUR PARENTS:**

I've decided to join the **Peace Corps!**

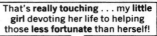

**WHAT YOU HOPE THEY WILL SAY:**

That's **really touching** . . . my **little girl** devoting her life to helping those **less fortunate** than herself!

WHAT YOU SAY TO YOUR PARENTS:

Someday, I'm gonna be the **President of the United States . . . !**

WHAT YOU HOPE THEY WILL SAY:

Son . . . I know you'll make a **fine** President . . . and you'll usher in **"The Great American Century"**!

**WHAT YOU SAY TO YOUR PARENTS:**

Boy... out of **two hundred applicants,** they picked **ME** for the **job!**

**WHAT YOU HOPE THEY WILL SAY:**

Son... if they'd had **two hundred THOUSAND** applicants, they **STILL** would have picked you!!

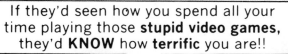

# WHAT THEY WILL PROBABLY SAY:

If they'd seen how you spend all your time playing those **stupid video games,** they'd **KNOW** how **terrific** you are!!

# The Lighter Side of **AFTERNOONS**

Artist & writer: Dave Berg

MAD ABOUT DAD

In addition to being stronger and wealthier than their children, parents have another big advantage in moments of conflict between generations. They have shelves of child psychology books to explain why their kids behave so badly. On the other hand, kids have never had even one parent psychology book to help them understand why Mom and Dad do all the kooky things they do. Until now, that is! Because that void is about to be filled with—

# The MAD Guide to Parental Hang-Ups...

Artist: Paul Cocker, Jr.    Writer: Tom Koch

## Parents Have A Hang-Up About...
## SCHOOL INTEGRATION

**They encourage you to make friends with classmates from minority groups . . . but they don't mean really close friends, like the kind you might bring home.**

## Parents Have A Hang-Up About...
## MAINTAINING TRADITIONS

**Like, your Dad wants everything about your college days to be exactly like his . . . except that you should get better grades and a better job offer at graduation time.**

## Parents Have A Hang-Up About...
## RADIOS

**They must always be played at low volume, and turned off completely by 11 P.M., except, of course, when the ball game Dad's listening to goes into extra innings.**

## Parents Have A Hang-Up About...
## THEIR MIXED EMOTIONS

**Which is why, when you're late, your Mom worries herself sick thinking you've been hurt in an accident, and then threatens to kill you when she finds out you haven't been.**

## Parents Have A Hang-Up About...
## ACCEPTING FAILURE

**That's why you get more pressure to become a Little League star right after Dad suddenly realizes he's becoming a middle-aged nobody!**

## Parents Have A Hang-Up About...
## MAKING MATURE DECISIONS

**Which may help you to understand why your father weighs the merits of all the new cars, and then decides to buy a Buick—because that's the kind his Daddy always had.**

## Parents Have A Hang-Up About...
## WOMEN'S LIB

**They don't mind if you want a career, just so you finish it quickly, land a desirable husband and start presenting them with Grandchildren.**

## Parents Have A Hang-Up About...
## CLEANLINESS

**In fact, the only thing that upsets them more than a dirty child is a dirty child who gets the bathroom dirty while he's getting himself clean.**

## Parents Have A Hang-Up About...
## SELF-ASSERTION

**They think you should stand right up in school and tell
your teacher to stop picking on you. "But, for heaven's
sake, don't ever tell her who advised you to do that!"**

## Parents Have A Hang-Up About...
## COMPETITIVE ACHIEVEMENT

**Which leads them to the strange belief that when you
win, this somehow proves that they're superior parents.**

# TO DAD— From a Businessman

Artist: George Woodbridge
Writer: Frank Jacobs

When I was just a little boy,
    You filled me with ambition—
And then you took me in the firm
    And gave me a position;
Secretly, behind your back,
    Your stock I have aquired;
I now own 51 per cent—
    And guess what, Dad?
    *You're fired!*